MW00907463

Copyright © 2021 by Luke Fredenberg

Illustrations © 2021 by Phillip Ortiz
Peel-creative.com / philliportiz.com

All rights reserved. No part of this publication may be reproduced, distributed, or transmitted in any form or by any means, including photocopying, recording, or other electronic or mechanical methods, without the prior written permission of the publisher, except in the case of brief quotations embodied in critical reviews and certain other noncommercial uses permitted by copyright law. For permission requests, write to the publisher, at the address below.

For questions, comments, or more information you can reach Luke at lukefredenberg@tprdfw.com

ISBN: 9780578320175

BRING-IT-TO-LIFE
PARTNERS

Creating this book has been a dream in my heart. This dream could not have been brought to life without the above-and-beyond generous support, encouragement, and investment of the following people.

A special thank you to:

Mark & Elizabeth Fredenberg

Bill & Becky Smith

Travis & Kristin Walker

Gabe & Brandy Lawless

Ryan Tilus

Bob & Barbara Dederich

TO ALL THE GROWN-UPS

We'll know for sure when we get there, but I believe the Bible says that the Church will go through the Great Tribulation in the days right before Jesus returns. These End Times will simultaneously be both the greatest hour for the Church, and the most difficult days that prepare us as a pure Bride who loves Jesus with every fiber of her being (Revelation 19:7-8, Matthew 22:37-38). I believe we should prepare our children because they may very well live through these days.

Jesus said, "In the world you will have tribulation. But take heart; I have overcome the world" (John 16:33). Through the difficulties of the Great Tribulation, which will include the rage of the nations against God and God's people (Psalm 2:1-3, Matthew 24:9), Jesus will never leave His people on their own, but promises to be with them through it all. He also promises that His Spirit of comfort and glory will rest on them (2 Corinthians 1:4, 1 Peter 4:14) even as difficulties mount.

I believe God's heart is to strengthen His Church with the nearness of His presence to remain steadfast through the most difficult of days, not loving their lives even unto death (Revelation 12:11). They will bear witness to Jesus with great boldness and power (Acts 4:29-31) and will do even greater signs and wonders than Jesus did (John 14:12) as a great revival sweeps across the Earth (Revelation 7:9-12, Isaiah 24:14-16).

If all of this is true and is coming soon, then it is of great importance to start talking, praying, and singing through these verses and others that describe life in the End Times. We want to stand boldly and faithfully with Jesus now and in the days ahead. I'm confident that if we lean into Him and ask for wisdom as we consider these things, He will give us more clarity.

Here's to the beginning of an incredible journey of the most epic adventure imaginable!

More teachings on the End Times available upon request.
Please email me at: LukeFredenberg@tprdfw.com.

THE BOY

IN TWO PLACES

WRITTEN BY LUKE FREDENBERG   ILLUSTRATED BY PHILLIP ORTIZ

As I look back upon the past,
On what my days were given to,

Life's not the same as it once
was. There's a new lens I'm
seeing it through.

John 16:33
I have said these things
to you, that in me you may
have peace. In the world
you will have tribulation.
But take heart; I have
overcome the world.

Matthew 24:6-7
And you will hear of wars and
rumors of wars. See that you
are not alarmed, for this must
take place, but the end is not
yet. For nation will rise against
nation, and kingdom against
kingdom, and there will be
famines and earthquakes in
various places.

My joy was in the shining sun,
Inviting me to come out and play.

I felt it soaring high on swings,
My friends and I at the park all day.

JOY

My joy is now when God comes near,
A smile spreads across my face.

I feel Him when I sing and pray.
I feel the love of His embrace.

I used to run in sun or rain,
Free as a bird to choose my way.
I ran in circles, having fun,
No plans, no goals, no cares all day.

My running now is purposeful;
I flee from evil close behind.
I run to where God's Spirit leads,
A place where darkness cannot find.

I once feared monsters in my room;
Night noises caused my mind to race.
Afraid of turning off the lights,
A flashlight near me just in case.

CHIRP! CHIRP!

CREAAAK

SNAP!

FEAR

Now, though terror is all around
God is the castle where I hide.
He says, "Fear not, for I am near."
His peace surrounds on every side.

EATING

I used to eat the whole day long,
Munching far beyond my share.
Never mindful of the ones
With bellies aching, cupboards bare.

SADNESS

Sadness once meant missing friends
When they were gone on family trips.
It once meant losing at a game,
With sour face and pouty lips.

Now it's missing martyred friends,
Who chose to give their lives away.
Faithful to the point of death,
They stand victorious with God today.

I used to sing along with songs,
Not knowing what their message was.
Loudly, proudly, belting out
Gibberish, nonsense, just because.

BLAH!

BLAH!

BLAH!

SING

PRAYER

I used to pray before a meal,
Or when Mom tucked me into bed.
A mindless string of others' words,
Barely knowing what I said.

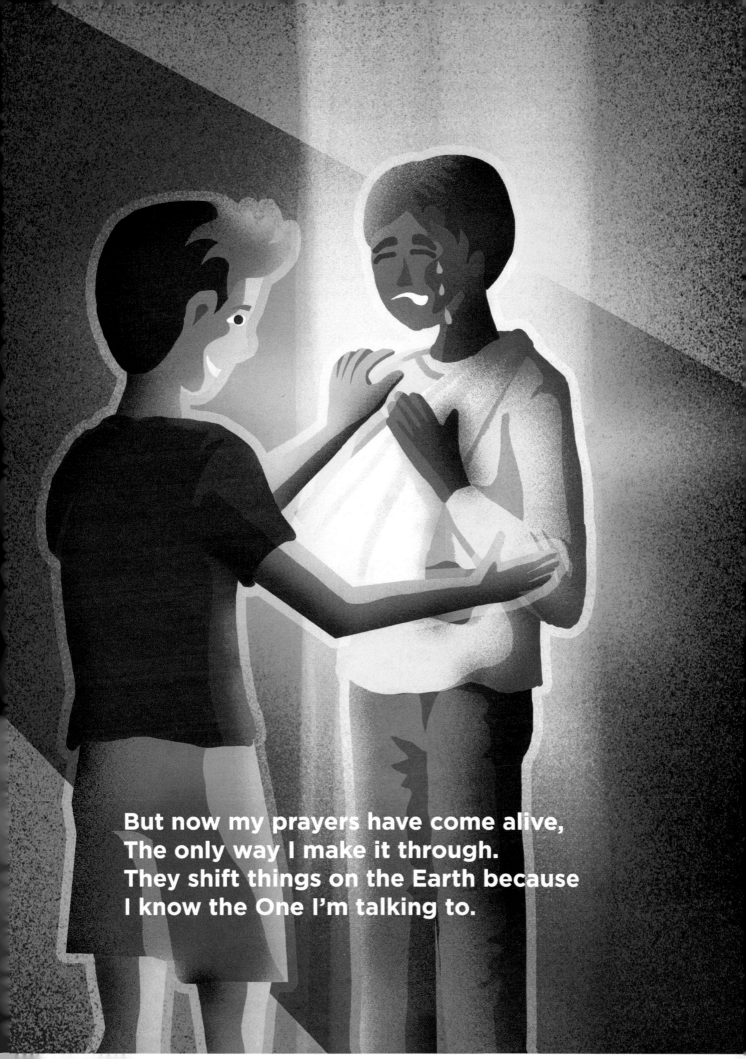

But now my prayers have come alive,
The only way I make it through.
They shift things on the Earth because
I know the One I'm talking to.

I used to hope Mom would forget,
Too busy to assign me chores.
I hoped I would find something sweet,
Buried deep in kitchen drawers.

Now my hope is in my King.
Jesus is coming back, I know.
He'll fight the evil here on Earth,
Delivering the final blow.

LIFE

Life used to be just having fun,
Ensuring I was never bored.
Always entertained, meanwhile,
The longings of my heart ignored.

Sure, now it's hard, and costly too,
But life has never been so sweet.
He's worth it all, my God, my Friend,
A real Man I soon will meet.

Made in the USA
Las Vegas, NV
19 November 2021

34835924R00019